IMAGES OF W

THE DESTRUCTION OF 6TH ARMY AT STALINGRAD

RARE PHOTOGRAPHS FROM WARTIME ARCHIVES

Ian Baxter

Pen & Sword

MILITARY

First published in Great Britain in 2020 by
PEN & SWORD MILITARY
An imprint of
Pen & Sword Books Ltd
47 Church Street
Barnsley
South Yorkshire
S70 2AS

ISBN 978-1-52674-795-2

Typeset by Concept, Huddersfield, West Yorkshire HD4 5JL
Printed and bound in England by CPI Group (UK) Ltd, Croydon, CR0 4YY

Pen & Sword Books Limited incorporates the imprints of Atlas, Archaeology, Aviation, Discovery, Family History, Fiction, History, Maritime, Military, Military Classics, Politics, Select, Transport, True Crime, Air World, Frontline Publishing, Leo Cooper, Remember When, Seaforth Publishing, The Praetorian Press, Wharncliffe Local History, Wharncliffe Transport, Wharncliffe True Crime and White Owl.

For a complete list of Pen & Sword titles please contact
PEN & SWORD BOOKS LIMITED
47 Church Street, Barnsley, South Yorkshire S70 2AS, England
E-mail: enquiries@pen-and-sword.co.uk
Website: www.pen-and-sword.co.uk

Contents

About the Author

Ian Baxter is a military historian who specialises in German twentieth-century military history. He has written more than fifty books including *Poland – The Eighteen Day Victory March*, *Panzers In North Africa*, *The Ardennes Offensive*, *The Western Campaign*, *The 12th SS Panzer-Division Hitlerjugend*, *The Waffen-SS on the Western Front*, *The Waffen-SS on the Eastern Front*, *The Red Army at Stalingrad*, *Elite German Forces of World War II*, *Armoured Warfare*, *German Tanks of War*, *Blitzkrieg*, *Panzer-Divisions at War*, *Hitler's Panzers*, *German Armoured Vehicles of World War Two*, *Last Two Years of the Waffen-SS at War*, *German Soldier Uniforms and Insignia*, *German Guns of the Third Reich*, *Defeat to Retreat: The Last Years of the German Army At War 1943–45*, *Operation Bagration – the Destruction of Army Group Centre*, *German Guns of the Third Reich*, *Rommel and the Afrika Korps*, *U-Boat War*, and most recently *The Sixth Army and the Road to Stalingrad*. He has written over a hundred articles including 'Last days of Hitler', 'Wolf's Lair', 'The Story of the V1 and V2 Rocket Programme', 'Secret Aircraft of World War Two', 'Rommel at Tobruk', 'Hitler's War With his Generals', 'Secret British Plans to Assassinate Hitler', 'The SS at Arnhem', 'Hitlerjugend', 'Battle of Caen 1944', 'Gebirgsjäger at War', 'Panzer Crews', 'Hitlerjugend Guerrillas', 'Last Battles in the East', 'The Battle of Berlin', and many more. He has also reviewed numerous military studies for publication, supplied thousands of photographs and important documents to various publishers and film production companies worldwide, and lectures to various schools, colleges and universities throughout the United Kingdom and the Republic of Ireland.

Introduction

Drawing on a superb collection of rare and unpublished photographs, this latest book in the popular Images of War Series provides an absorbing insight into the last months of General Paulus' 6th Army on the Eastern Front. In dramatic detail it analyses the 6th Army's advance through southern Russia in May 1942 when it began its summer offensive – Operation Blue. It describes its arrival on the River Don three months later, followed by its drive to the banks of the River Volga, north of the city of Stalingrad. It was here in Stalingrad that every Russian soldier was determined to fight to the death. What was to follow was a battle of unrivalled scale where the 6th Army were drawn into a bloody and costly urban battle of attrition. This book shows how the 6th Army tried in desperation to capture the city, but was constantly beaten back by stubborn enemy resistance. Slowly, the 6th Army found itself surrounded, trapped in what became known as the cauldron, and some 265,000 men, many Rumanian, were exposed daily to the full blast of Russian artillery, and to frostbite and dysentery, with no way to escape.

The Germans performed a number of attempted relief operations, one under the command of Field Marshal Erich von Manstein. With in-depth captions and rare photographs, this book shows vehicles and men from Manstein's relief operation, Winter Storm. In the deep snow Manstein attempted to reach the cauldron to relieve the 6th Army. But the relief effort failed and the 6th Army was forced to continue fighting to the death. Eventually its last remnants were either destroyed or surrendered, and the once fearsome fighting machine that had boldly advanced across the steppe the previous summer was but a shadow of its former self.

Prelude to Destruction

For the invasion of Russia that was unleashed on 22 June 1941, the Germans divided their forces into three Army Groups: North, under Field Marshal Ritter von Leeb; Centre, under Field Marshal Fedor von Bock; and South, under Field Marshal Gerd von Rundstedt.

On the southern front Rundstedt's six infantry divisions with some 600 tanks distributed among them smashed its way through thinly held Russia defences. The main thrust in the south was directed between the southern edge of the Pripet Marshes and the foothills of the Carpathian Mountains. Here Rundstedt concentrated the whole of the 1st Panzer Army, 6th Army, and 17th Army. The 6th Army under the command of Field Marshal von Reichenau consisted of four Army Corps and one reserve. Within days the 6th Army successfully drove Soviet forces back and cut them off in the wooded swampland between the marshes and the mountains. As it pushed on towards the Dnieper River it continued to cut off enemy formations. By August it had swung east of Kiev and begun mopping up the last pockets of resistance around the besieged city. When the battle of Kiev ended on 21 September 1941, almost 665,000 Russian troops had been captured in the encirclement.

Many of the 6th Army's units were not mechanized. Some 25,000 horses were used to move guns and supplies. This type of transportation was initially acceptable, but by the time the army arrived at the higher Donets River in October 1941 the weather began to change. Cold driving rain turned the Russian countryside into a quagmire with roads and fields becoming virtually impassable. Many of the roads leading to the Caucasus via Rostov had become boggy swamps. Tanks and other tracked vehicles managed to push through the mire at slow pace, animal draft, trucks and other wheeled vehicles became hopelessly stuck in deep boggy mud. During November, German supply lines became increasingly overstretched, their vehicles breaking down and casualty returns mounting. Stiff enemy resistance too began to hinder progress. As the situation deteriorated Rundstedt, against Hitler's orders, ordered Kleist's 1st Panzer Army to evacuate Rostov and fall back over the Mius River, some sixty miles west of the city. On the night of 30 November Rundstedt was relieved of his command of the 6th Army and replaced by Reichenau, and then a few days later he was replaced by a staff officer named Friedrich Paulus. For some time the 43-year-old Paulus had been wanting a field post and was elated when he received his new assignment.

On 1 January 1942, Paulus was promoted to general of panzer troops and took up his new command four days later. He had been a highly efficient, fastidious staff officer, and regarded Hitler as a flawless military expert.

From his staff vehicle Paulus directed his first battle as commander of the 6th Army along the Dnieper River in the area around Dnepropetrovsk. It was here in freezing temperatures that Army Group South halted strong Soviet attacks and brought the winter offensive in the southern sector to a grinding halt. Both sides were totally exhausted following weeks of ceaseless fighting. While the front lines stagnated the 6th Army engaged in a race for supplies.

On 9 May the German lines once more erupted in flame and smoke as the Russians unleashed a spring attack at Volchansk. The main strike came three days later when 640,000 men and 1,200 tanks from Timoshenko's Ukrainian Army attacked the 6th Army and pushed it back in the direction of Kharkov. On 15 May, Red Army forces threatened to envelope the city from the north and south. Paulus's 6th Army had been severely battered by the ferocity of the enemy as it tried frantically to hold its positions. Paulus had only ten infantry divisions, a Hungarian light division and a Slovak artillery regiment. For two days these forces were subjected to incessant attacks until 1st Panzer and 17th Armies were able to relieve the pressure. On 20 May Paulus was able to counter-attack east of Kharkov, and within a few days successfully linked up with Kleist west of the city and encircled the main Russian striking force.

The success at Kharkov brought new optimism to the ranks of the German army. Paulus received the Knights Cross for his part in the victory, and a number of other commanders too were decorated. Though the Red Army had made a formidable impression on Paulus, he was nonetheless convinced, as was his Führer, that victory in the south would be secured. Yet, even as his troops pulled out east of Kharkov to take part in the drive to Voronezh and the clearing operations of the Don, he never envisaged that the first seeds were being sewn of something more terrible than anything that his troops, or indeed the Wehrmacht, had ever experienced.

Chapter One

The Road to Hell

By the spring of 1942 Hitler was now in full command of the army and was determined to obliterate the Soviet army in southern Russia once and for all. To finally destroy his enemy a plan had been worked out for an all-out drive south to capture a city that bore than name of Stalin. Stalingrad comprised approximately 500,000 inhabitants and stretched for 12 miles along the west bank of the Volga. It was the third largest industrial city in Russia and boasted a huge tractor plant which had been converted to produce more than a quarter of the country's tanks and armoured vehicles. There was a gun factory, metallurgical and chemical works, railroads, and oil tank farms. The Russians used the river for the shipment of oil from the Caucasus.

Within four days Voronezh was captured sending Red Army troops reeling back across the vast Russian steppe for their lives. Following the capture of the city the 4th Panzer Army then swung south-east along the Don where it linked up with Paulus's 6th Army east of Kharkov. Over the next few weeks, strung out over more than 200 miles, the 6th Army with twenty divisions – 250,000 men, 500 panzers, 7,000 guns and mortars, and 25,000 horses – pushed down the Don corridor towards Stalingrad.

On 17 July two of Paulus's divisions entered the town of Bobovskaya on the upper Chir and then drove east making their way steadily towards the Don. A few days later, with victory beckoning, Paulus received a 'Hitler Order' instructing 6th Army to advance on Stalingrad and capture it by high-speed assault. Paulus's troops had been marching continuously for almost two weeks and were exhausted. Nonetheless, he made a determined effort to destroy the defences of the 62nd and 64th Soviet armies. In some areas there was bitter opposition and the Russians managed to hold Serafimovich and Kremenskaya.

In front of Stalingrad German soldiers were becoming increasingly aware of stiffer enemy resistance. Units of the 6th Army were now compelled to consolidate so that they could push forward and commit their whole strength against Stalingrad. Paulus was directed to smash his way to the west of the Don. From here they would press onto the Volga and into Stalingrad where it was believed the troops would easily destroy the last vestiges of resistance holding out inside the smouldering city.

The drive to Stalingrad was codenamed Operation Brunswick, and was conducted by Paulus's 6th Army supported by General Hoth's 4th Panzer Army. The main plan was for these two armies to converge at speed into Stalingrad, occupy the city and then block enemy communications between the Don and Volga. However, as German soldiers stood poised to strike across the west bank of the river, the Russians were frantically making preparations not to evacuate the area, but to defend their beloved city with every last drop of their blood.

On 22 August, soldiers of the 6th Army completed erecting their pontoon bridges across the Don and began sending advance elements of General Hube's 16th Panzer Division across the broad expanse of water to the east bank. Early the following morning Count von Strachwitz's Abteilung of the 2nd Panzer Regiment, reinforced with Panzergrenadier companies, advanced forward from the Don towards the Volga.

Although there was sporadic enemy resistance, by the afternoon of 23 August parts of the 16th Panzer Division reached the banks of the Volga north of Stalingrad. However, by this stage the whole region around Stalingrad had prepared itself for the defence of the city. All non-combatants men, women and children — nearly 200,000 of them — were drafted in to build defensive positions in and around the city, in spite of incessant Luftwaffe attacks.

While Stalingrad was bombed from the air, the 16th Panzer Division began digging in along the banks of the Volga and its commanders made their final plans to attack the city.

Early on 24 August, 'Group Drumpen' of the 16th Panzer Division launched an attack against Spartakovka, north of the industrial part of the city. The Germans expected an easy victory, but as they pushed along the northern outskirts they were repulsed by strong Russian resistance. A number of panzers then attempted to storm the city from the west, but they were soon halted by Russian tanks and infantry.

The Red Army's main objective was to force the Germans to abandon their corridor between the Don and Volga. Over the next few days they made a number of concerted attacks against the 6th Army dug in along the shores. Russian artillery shelling and fighter aircraft attacks were particularly heavy. Conditions in the German trenches had deteriorated, and when it rained almost continuously on 29 August their improvised shelters soon filled with water. Only days earlier these soldiers had been elated by being the first to reach the riverbank. Now they were crouched in drenched shelters among shattered trees and smouldering craters. Though it was a miserable existence, worse was to come.

A portrait photograph of General Wilhelm Ernst Paulus, commander of the 6th Army. Paulus was a truly proficient, fastidious staff officer, but he regarded Hitler as a flawless military expert, which would become his undoing in the battle of Stalingrad.

A 3.7cm anti-tank gun crewman can be seen carrying two cans of ammunition to his gun position during the opening phase of Operation Blue, the summer offensive south through Russia.

Part of an infantry regiment pausing in their march south. An average infantry regiment in 1942 comprised 3,250 soldiers, a staff, a horse- or bicycle-mounted reconnaissance section, and pioneer and signal platoons.

A light Horch cross country vehicle crosses a shallow river. For these soldiers advancing through southern Russia that summer the environment for many was totally alien. Often it was not the enemy that was the problem, but the countryside. It was also often very hot, and some regiments ran seriously short of water.

A light Horch country vehicle with commanding officers inside halted on a dusty road. Motorcycle riders can be seen in support to protect it from possible enemy attack.

A prime mover is towing a 15cm s.FH18 along a dusty road. A typical German infantry division possessed an artillery regiment with three light and one heavy battery. The light batteries comprised thirty-six guns, including the 10.5cm l.FH18. The heavy battery contained twelve guns, being the robust and powerful 15cm s.FH18. These guns would be used along the banks of the Don and Volga to soften enemy targets.

Two squad leaders armed with the MP40 machine pistol, which was one of the most effective sub-machine guns ever produced.

An interesting photograph showing two signalmen operating a portable radio. This was the standard radio used at battalion and regimental level. Often a radio team were attached to a company for semi-independent missions, such as reconnaissance duties. These devices were carried in two cases (transmitter and receiver), but could not be operated on the move.

On the march and infantry can be seen with a single-axle twin-machine-gun wagon. The wagon could be either towed by motor vehicle or animal draught. Production of these steel wagons was discontinued by 1943. The two 7.92mm MG34s mounted on the wagon could be easily dismounted and fired from their integral bipods or from the Lafette 34 mount tripods.

Infantrymen on the march through a field. During this period of the war the average German soldier was well equipped. Wearing their trademark M35 steel helmet, they can be seen wearing their support straps and carrying two sets of ammunition pouches for a total of sixty rounds for their carbine. They are also equipped with their rain cape/shelter quarter, an entrenching tool, a bread bag for rations and a gasmask canister. A small backpack was also provided for spare clothing, personal items, and additional rations along with a satchel-like spare clothing bag.

Advancing during the summer of 1942 and infantry of the 6th Army pass a Russian village. Note the soldier carrying his MG34 on his shoulder. The distances over which these soldiers marched were immense, but the weather was good and resistance was minimal, so many miles could be covered each day.

An interesting photograph showing the common use of a rifle sling being placed over the shoulders and around the neck. This method of carrying helped relieve the considerable weight of the ammunition cans when being moved by the infantry from one place to another.

An MG34 team which was part of a rifle group. The gunner can be seen on the left and carries the MG34 along with the tool and spare parts pouch. The number two gunner carries most of the ammunition, while the number three carries the spare barrels and another ammunition can.

An interesting photograph showing an NCO armed with an MP40 machine pistol being carried over his right shoulder. His personal equipment can clearly be identified. Between his mess kit and gas mask canister is a binocular case. He can also be seen carrying a folded up shelter cape or *Zeltbahn* and his water canister. The oval-shaped item on the back of his collar is a leather eyepiece cover for his binoculars.

During the 6th Army's drive, the initial stages of the summer offensive was very successful with many Russian soldiers that had not withdrawn being encircled or destroyed. In this photograph a Soviet soldier has surrendered to a German infantry unit. They are still ready to rise to their feet just in case of surrounding enemy fire.

(**Opposite, above**) On the march south are infantry belonging to the 6th Army. For these soldiers many had never experienced such vast open spaces, with huge tracts of land devoid of any habitation. Much of their drive towards the Don River consisted of nothing but vast flat plains, wheat and sunflower fields, and dusty roads.

(**Opposite, below**) A prime mover towing what appears to be a trailer for a bridging section. Note how the road has been turned into a quagmire following a downpour.

(**Above**) Photographed from another vehicle advancing south is a Pz.Kpfw.III moving along a dusty road.

(**Opposite, above**) Infantry are inside a Russian town armed with the Karbine 98K bolt action rifle. One of the soldiers can clearly be seen injured and being assisted by his comrade. While the 6th Army drive south to the Don was rapid, regiments did sometimes come up against Russian resistance.

(**Opposite, below**) Various vehicles belonging to the 6th Army consisting mainly of halftracks towing PaK guns to the forward edge of the battlefield. Note in the distance a battery of 15cm field howitzers with one of them already embroiled in firing against an enemy target.

(**Above**) A troop leader gives instructions to his men before resuming their advance. The rifleman or *Schütze* pictured on the right can be seen wearing the complete kit. His trademark model 1935 steel helmet is worn, which provided protection while marching to the battlefront and during combat. His leather belt with support straps carried two sets of three ammunition pouches for a total of sixty rounds for his carbine. The soldier also wears his combat harness for his mess kit and special camouflage rain cape or *Zeltbahn*. He is also wearing an entrenching tool, and attached to the entrenching tool carrier is a bayonet, a bread bag for rations, a gas mask canister which is slung over the shoulder, and an anti-gas cape in its pouch attached to the shoulder strap. The infantryman's flashlight, though not seen, was normally attached to the tunic, and inside the tunic pocket he carried wound dressings. A small backpack was issued to the soldiers, though some did not wear them. The backpack was intended for spare clothing, personal items, and additional rations along with a spare clothing satchel.

An infantryman armed with his Karbiner 98K and seen with a stick grenade in his black leather belt is escorting a column of Russian prisoners along a road to the rear.

Soldiers take cover at the side of a road during some fighting. In the distance plumes of smoke can be seen rising in the air, signifying artillery bombardments. During July 1942 strung out over more than 200 miles the 6th Army with twenty divisions – 250,000 men, 500 panzers, 7,000 guns and mortars, and 25,000 horses – pushed down towards the Don corridor on Stalingrad. The tremendous distances which these divisions had to cover could only be achieved by long foot marches.

Refugees sit in a field with their cart and horses. Along the road as far as the eye can see is a column of infantry support vehicles carrying soldiers to the front.

Hundreds of Russian prisoners and what appear to be Russian civilians are marched along a road to the rear during the German drive in July 1942.

Two infantrymen pose for the camera armed with their Karbiner 98k bolt action rifles. They both are well armed with the Stg24 stick grenades which have been secured inside their leather belts.

A Pz.Kpfw.III has halted on a road. During the drive south, due to the lack of adequate rail and road links, natural obstacles such as the *balka* (steep-sided, dried-up watercourses) often obstructed the advance of a tank column until a diversion was made or a bridge erected. Sometimes the advance was hampered by lack of fuel, which had been temporarily diverted to Army Group A. Nonetheless, despite the problems, 6th Army during the first half of July made good progress.

Halted on a road are Luftwaffe personnel standing next to an 8.8cm flak gun being towed by a prime mover. The gun's high muzzle velocity and flat trajectory made it accurate and effective against both aircraft and tanks. These guns are positioned for air defence. They were lethal to enemy aircraft.

A stationary Pz.Kpfw.III is having its wheels worked on out in the hot Russian steppe. One of the crew members is drinking from his canteen bottle.

A shirtless radio operator can be seen communicating. Note the transmitter and receiver on top of each other, which were carried in two cases.

A commanding officer is conferring with one of his men at a hastily erected command post out in the field. Note the waterproof *Zeltbahn* shelter quarter next to them.

Two smiling crew members on board a halftrack towing what appears to be a PaK gun along a road to the front.

Another photograph showing a halftrack towing an 8.8cm flak gun, this time across rougher terrain. The 8.8cm flak gun was used extensively during the crossing of the Don and along the banks of the Volga where they were prominently positioned to attack enemy shipping and aircraft.

A prime mover is hauling an 8.8cm flak gun along a dusty road. The '88' could be fired while mounted on its limbers, but it was less accurate to do so and the rate of fire was less.

Marching towards the front infantrymen can be seen passing through a village. The soldier nearest has an MG34 machine gun slung over his shoulder. Locals can be seen watching.

During the summertime in Russia, especially in dense overgrowth and water, mosquitoes plagued the troops. In this photograph an MG34 squad march along a small stagnant stream. The soldier leading his men wears a mosquito net over his M35 steel helmet.

(**Opposite, above**) Soldiers can be seen hauling a PaK35/36 across rough terrain to another position. This weapon was the standard anti-tank gun of the *Landser* during the early part of the war. The gun weighed only 432kg and had sloping splinter shield. It fired a solid shot round at a muzzle velocity of 2,500 feet per second with a maximum range of 4km.

(**Opposite, below**) Russian PoWs being led along a road to the rear following their capture. As German forces drove deeper towards the Don River enemy resistance grew. Thousands of Red Army troops that did not withdraw were encircled, captured or destroyed.

(**Above**) A long column of soldiers belonging to an unidentified regiment of the 6th Army march towards the front. Much of the German army's advance, even in 1942, was still undertaken by animal draft which carried ammunition, suppliers and soldiers.

An interesting photograph showing a horse-drawn column pulling what appears to be supplies to the front. Among the column are motorcycle combinations which have halted on the muddy road.

Any means for soldiers to hitch a lift on board vehicles bound for the front was a welcome relief. In this photograph soldiers are clinging to a light Horch cross country vehicle.

A photograph showing a group of Russian women the troops have come across while advancing along a road. These women were often pressed into service as personnel assisting German troops with collecting water and food.

A Russian armoured vehicle can be seen burning on a road inside a town. As the 6th Army advanced further south the Red Army withdrew luring the Germans ever deeper into enemy terrain.

Soldiers converse before a truck carrying troops departs for the front.

An infantryman observes a dead Russian soldier sprawled in a ditch by the road during his unit's drive to the front.

A close-up view of what appears to be a motorcyclist wearing the distinctive aviator goggles. He wears the standard infantryman's tunic and M38 field cap. Note his torch attached on his left jacket. He wears a scarf around his neck to protect his mouth and nose while driving along the dusty roads and fields.

(**Above**) A column of armoured vehicles including halftracks advance along a road. The leading halftrack has straw attached to help camouflage it from both air and ground surveillance.

(**Opposite, above**) An excellent photograph showing an MG34 squad marching towards a village. The team are well supplied and wear full battle kit for their long march.

(**Opposite, below**) Commanding officers can be seen standing next to a Horch cross country vehicle conferring. Moving past is a column of wheeled vehicles and carts being hauled by animals. An average artillery regiment was authorised to contain some 2,500 troops and 2,274 horses, the latter of which drew over 200 wagons and artillery caissons.

The drive south in the summer of 1942 was particularly hot and demanding for the infantry. In this photograph a group of soldiers are drinking from a waterhole.

A fire mission with a PaK35/36 gun positioned on a farmstead gun. A typical infantry regiment controlled three infantry battalions, an infantry gun company with six 7.5cm l.IG18 and two 15cm s.IG33 guns, and an anti-tank company with twelve 3.7cm PaK35/36 guns.

(**Opposite, above**) Infantry including an MG34 machine gunner can be seen crossing a stream by an old wooden bridge.

(**Opposite, below**) A pontoon bridge has been erected over the Don and armour and weaponry are being transported across. Note the prime mover towing the 15cm howitzer across the bridge.

(**Above**) A column of horse-drawn carts being transported towards the Volga. Many hundreds of thousands of horses died either due to combat action, the extreme weather or lack of forage, and many were eaten by starving soldiers at Stalingrad.

Chapter Two

The Siege of Stalingrad

On 29 August General Hoth's 4th Panzer Army launched a new attack from Abganerovo that saw his units clash with the Russian 64th and 62nd Armies. A few days later, 2 September, Paulus ordered his panzers to make contact with Hoth's force to attempt to cut off the two Russian armies and destroy them. But by the time the two German armies made contact, the bulk of the Russian troops had withdrawn into Stalingrad. Supported by continuous aerial attacks, advanced elements of the 6th Army made a series of probing attacks into Stalingrad, while the 4th Panzer Army closed in on its southern outskirts.

Two days later, 4 September, Hoth's forces attacked units of the 64th Russian Army. Battles raged all day and within twenty-four hours 14th Panzer reported it had successfully captured Kuporosnoye, a suburb of Stalingrad. It appeared Stalingrad would soon fall and, under heavy fire, the Germans began smashing a route through the city for the main attacking force of the 6th Army.

A week later, 13 September, two shock forces of the 6th Army attacked through the southern half of the city, and there followed a bitter bloody battle of attrition. Though the Russians were outnumbered, they were masters of house-to-house combat. They had developed a system of killing zones, in which small Russians units were ordered to defend every square yard to the death if necessary. They were armed with machine guns, mortars, grenades, flame throwers and explosive charges.

The Germans slowly made their way through the burning city at huge cost. On the northern edge of the city there was a huge grain elevator, and during the third week of September the Germans pounded the building incessantly for three days with artillery, setting it on fire. During the night of 20 September the elevator was captured and fighting soon moved to Red Square, to a nail factory and the Univermag department store. Over the next few days bitter fighting was often hand-to-hand. Losses on both sides were extremely high, and the fighting continued.

By 22 September the whole of Stalingrad was a sea of flame and smoke. In the north of the city between Orlovka and Rynok the XVI Panzer Division were engaged. Further south the 71st, 76th, 100th, and 295th infantry divisions fought against the 62nd Army along the railway line and the Mechetka River near Gorodishche. South of the city the XXIV Panzer Division, XXIX Motorized Division and the XIV Panzer Division made a series of deep penetrations against the 64th Army.

But by the end of September the Germans had still not captured the city. The 3rd Rumanian Army were ordered to take over Paulus's front west of the Don and protect his flanks. However, the Rumanian soldiers were ill-equipped, short of rations and lacking adequate winter clothing, and their front lines collapsed against Red Army attacks. It took Hoth's 4th Panzer Army to wheel into action to prevent the complete devastation of the front.

Meanwhile inside Stalingrad the fighting continued. In the first six weeks since Paulus's 6th Army moved from the Don, 7,700 soldiers had been killed and 31,000 wounded. Around 10 per cent of his army had been destroyed. In one division the infantry battalions had an average of three officers, eleven NCOs, and only sixty-two men. Ammunition too was dwindling and they were in desperate need of resupply. Nevertheless, Paulus continued to attack. Halftracks were used to carry grenadiers, but they were open-topped and lightly armoured, and were vulnerable to close-quarters attack. Panzer and assault guns too were more vulnerable when in the city.

On 14 October Paulus sent five divisions against the Barrikady gun factory and the tractor factory. By midnight they had surrounded the tractor plant, but at a high price. Some 3,500 men had been wounded or killed in the fighting. Further casualties fell as the Germans tried to hold on to their positions in the rubble.

While this was going on, Russian reinforcements from other parts of the country were being moved towards Stalingrad. Hungarian, Italian, and Rumanian forces allied to the Germans were expected to defend their positions against these new Russian formations advancing towards the city. But they were ill-equipped, badly trained, and were beginning to desert or withdraw from their lines at the least sign of fighting.

On 23 October the Germans held the tractor factory and most of the Barrikady gun factory, while the Red Army held the Red October Factory. Two days later the Germans had captured the centre of Spartakovka and the 6th Army nearly reached the Volga. The next day they were pushed back with major losses, but undeterred the German 100th Infantry Division used artillery to blast its way through Russian positions and got to within firing range of the last remaining Russian ferry landing on the western bank of the river. The Germans were sure that victory was imminent. They now held nine-tenths of the city – the Russians were left with about 6 miles of the Volga riverbank a few hundred yards wide. Their situation was dire, but they were holding out. What now worried the Germans was the onset of winter.

(**Opposite, above**) Infantry advance across a field at the ready armed with Stg24 stick grenades. This suggests that the area is infested with enemy troops, and at a moment's notice these men will throw themselves to the ground preparing to use their weapons.

(**Opposite, below**) An 8cm sGrW 34 mortar crew on the advance. Each battalion fielded six of these excellent mortars. At Stalingrad in both defence and attack the mortar would earn a reputation that its valuable high explosive capability far outranged that of rifles or hand grenades.

(**Opposite, above**) Infantry advance towards the Don. In the distance smoke can be seen rising in the air along the banks of the river.

(**Opposite, below**) A column of support vehicles can be seen advancing along a road bound for the front. Black smoke can be seen rising.

(**Above**) Captured Russian troops are sitting waiting to be moved to the rear. Note the two soldiers to the left of the photograph. These were known as *Feldgendarmerie*. Once German forces had occupied an area, various administrative organizations were moved into the occupied zone, and these included military policemen, or *Feldgendarmerie*. Note both troops are wearing the standard German army M1936 service uniform with the dull aluminum Gorget plate suspended around the neck by a chain.

(**Opposite, above**) As 6th Army units push forward towards the Don, Russian soldiers that had not kept pace with their own regiments and withdrawn over the river were quickly encircled, destroyed or captured. In this photograph Red Army troops have surrendered and are being searched by their captors.

(**Opposite, below**) Approaching Stalingrad and soldiers can be seen with fixed bayonets examining Russian dugouts in the city's outer defences. Thousands of dugouts, shelters and improvised defensive positions and trenches were constructed in front of Stalingrad by the Red Army between the Rivers Don and Volga.

(**Above**) Infantry march along a road passing a crude defensive position that the Russians had erected across the road. Note the signalman carrying one of the radios on his back.

A German soldier armed with his Karbiner 98k bolt action rifle can be seen approaching a vehicle that is on fire after presumably being knocked out of action.

Between the Don and Volga Rivers the Russians had dug various defensive positions including anti-tank ditches. In the photograph an infantryman can be seen riding his bicycle along one of the numerous anti-tank ditches that stretched in front of Stalingrad.

Motorcycles and a Pz.Kpfw.III can be seen operating in a field approaching the Don River in late July 1942.

(**Opposite, above**) Following an exchange of enemy fire a German soldier can be seen aiding one of his comrades. Next to them is a Russian soldier who presumably has just been captured but is still clutching an ammunition box.

(**Opposite, below**) Russian PoWs have been contained in a makeshift holding area and are awaiting their fate. Often the soldiers were starved to death or executed. Those deemed fit for labour were transported back through Poland and worked, often to death, in labour or concentration camps.

(**Above**) A troop leader can be seen armed with the famous 9mm MP40, commonly known by the men as the *Schmeisser*. Often squad leaders were issued with these weapons. This particular soldier is carrying seven 32-round magazines, one on the weapon and three spares in each of the two magazine pouches. Note he has a number of Stg24 stick hand grenades carried in his infantryman's black leather belt.

An excellent photograph showing assault troops preparing to advance from their position wearing full battle kit. The soldier in the foreground carries a cartridge case M1941 for his MG34 machine gun, seen in the background. The infantryman standing in the centre carries an ammunition can and containers for two spare machine-gun barrels.

Soldiers and their commanders confer before resuming their drive on Stalingrad. Three of the men can be seen looking skyward as there apparently appears to be aerial activity.

Two photographs taken in sequence showing a forward artillery observer position near the Don River in July or August. To detect and determine the location of their enemy they have the 6 × 30 Sf.14Z scissor periscope. Forward observers like this were assigned to artillery batteries. Communications between observer posts and the firing battery was usually done by field telephone and sometimes radio.

An infantryman poses for the camera near the banks of the Don in a captured Russian foxhole. These positions were very difficult to detect as they were often camouflaged with saplings or vegetation.

Here riflemen armed with their 98k carbine bolt action rifles are positioned in a firing trench. These short slit trenches were typically dug between one and four metres forward from a standard trench, and provided a better offensive or defensive position.

From a dugout a soldier
surveyors the battlefield
through a pair of binoculars.
Note the Stg24 stick grenade
next to him.

Russian PoWs being escorted
through undergrowth to the
rear from where they will be
assembled and most probably
transported west to a labour
camp and worked to death.

Mortar troops rest during a pause in the fighting with their well dug-in 8cm sGrW 34 mortar. It was common for infantry, especially during longer periods of action, to fire their mortar from trenches or dug-in positions where crews would be better protected from enemy fire.

The workhorse of the infantry division was the Sd.Kfz.251 seen here transporting troops to the forward edge of the battlefield. On the eastern front the halftrack undoubtedly transformed the fighting quality of the infantry and enabled the soldiers to advance with less difficulty.

Commanding officers in a forward observation post deducing the whereabouts of the enemy and planning their next move.

At a forward observation post, a soldier peers through a set of 6 × 30 Sf.14Z scissor binoculars connected on a tripod. They were nicknamed 'donkey ears' by the troops. Each artillery battery had an observation post among the frontline positions.

A PaK35/36 positioned on the banks of the Don. Even though the PaK35/36 had become inadequate for operational needs in the face of growing armoured opposition by 1942, they were still quite capable of causing serious damage to their opponent.

A lull on the front lines and an artillery man belonging to an unidentified 15cm field howitzer battery can be seen resting. The 15cm howitzers are seen in their elevated position. This particular gun was primarily designed to attack targets deeper in the enemy's rear. This included command posts, reserve units, assembly areas, and logistics facilities.

(**Above & opposite above**) Two photographs of a flak crew beside a 2cm FlaK30 position. The 2cm FlaK30 was a very effective weapon and was operated by only two men. Although these weapons were used extensively against aerial attack they were, as this photo illustrates, used against ground targets as well.

(**Opposite, below**) A German soldier at a field post with a typewriter. Note the bunker installation. Many of these bunkers, which were known by the troops as small houses, were often built along the front.

(**Above**) A rifle group can be seen manning a defensive position along a rail line embankment. Each group possessed an MG34 light machine gun around which its base of fire was built. The rifle group was divided into two troops.

(**Opposite, above**) On the outskirts of the city and a Pz.Kpfw.III can be seen rolling through a village. Note the Pz.Kpfw.IV concealed next to a house.

(**Opposite, below**) Infantrymen pause near a crater before attacking the enemy. The second soldier from the left carries a canvas rucksack. By 1943, the infantry found the traditional flat rucksack insufficient for carrying gear.

Soldiers advance from open ground during a counter-attack. The infantryman leading the attack is more than likely a squad leader and is armed with an MP38 or MP40 machine pistol. The soldier to the far right has a Walther P38 pistol while the remainder of the troop are armed with Mauser Kar98k carbines.

A soldier prepares to throw a Stg24 stick hand grenade in what appears to be a staged attack. This was the standard hand grenade used by both *Heerestruppen* and Waffen-SS during the war. It was armed by unscrewing a cap on the end of the handle, pulling a cord which activated an igniter, and then it was thrown to detonate. The user had 4.5 seconds to throw the weapon before it exploded.

Infantrymen board a small inflatable boat on the Don. These boats were capable of carrying three or four men. Note that one of the soldiers inside the boat is armed with a Czech 7.92mm vz.26 light machine gun.

An MG34 crew can be seen during an attack in what appears to be a propaganda photograph. The MG34 has its bipod fully extended, allowing the gunner to throw down his weapon at a moment's notice and start firing.

Positioned in a log-bunker is an MG34 machine gun. Throughout the war, and especially during urban defensive fighting, the Germans often constructed wide firing ports in bunkers to allow a broad field of fire.

A signalman is operating a portable radio (*Tornisterfunkgerät* or *TornFu*). This was the standard radio system used at battalion and regimental level. The signals provided both field and radio communications support within the division, linking all subordinate units.

An infantryman armed with his Karbiner 98K bolt action rifle rests before resuming his advance. Note his Stg24 stick grenade, more than likely secured inside his black leather infantryman's belt.

Infantry advance towards to the Volga, approaching a number of knocked-out T-34 tanks, presumably deployed in the field to stall the German drive to the river and allow its own units to withdraw and take up defensive positions.

An interesting photograph showing a Luftwaffe flak crew positioned to overlook the Volga preparing their weapon for enemy contact.

(**Above**) An MG34 gun crew on the march through some trees on the way to the front. Note the crewmember carrying the tripod mount, or Lafette 34, on his back. A typical heavy machine gun troop was provided with the Lafette 34, a pair of leather carrying slings (*Trageriemen*), a long-range optical sight (*Zeileinrichtung* 34), at least two spare barrel carriers (*Laufbehalter* 34), belt filling device (*Gurtfuller* 34), a number of 300-round metal cartridge cases, and various items of cleaning equipment.

(**Opposite, above**) Infantry together with a light MG34 machine gun troop are protecting themselves behind an elevated part of a field. In German the term 'light' defined the role and not the weight of the machine gun. The MG34 had tremendous staying power against enemy infantry, and troops, especially during the battle actually inside Stalingrad.

(**Opposite, below**) What appears to be a forward artillery observation post and an observer estimates the range to a target using a 6x30 Sf 14Z Scherenfernrohr (scissor binoculars). Observers looked for weapon muzzles, moving infantry, armoured vehicles, fires, smoke from cooking and anything else they could detect to locate their enemy.

(**Above & opposite, above**) A sad spectacle: two photographs of dejected Soviet PoWs. The first shows PoWs in a temporary camp. The second shows them trudging along a road with an injured soldier being hauled along by a cart and another wounded comrade behind him being stretchered. They wear a variety of standard infantry clothing including the greatcoat, the quilted winter jacket, and the M1935 pattern field uniform, which was made from cotton material for summer operations. Many of the troops are wearing the standard infantryman's field cap, which was commonly used by the soldiers in preference to their heavy M1940 helmet.

(**Opposite, below**) Support vehicles are seen crossing a pontoon bridge erected across the Don to bring supplies to the front as quickly as possible.

A different part of the Don with various support vehicles and a motorcycle combination approaching the west bank of the river in July 1942.

A photo taken just before a 15cm s.FH18 is fired. This weapon was the standard piece in a division and use of artillery was a necessity to any ground force engaging an enemy. Infantry together with motorised artillery became the backbone of the fighting in the early years on the Russian front.

Infantry have dug in during their advance from the Don to the Volga. The soil was usually piled enemy side, but these troops have piled the earth completely around their position.

An infantryman sits next to his shelter near the Volga River. These *Halbgruppenunterstande*, or half-group living bunkers, gave the men some protection from enemy fire as well as from the often harsh Russian weather.

(**Opposite, above**) Troops have taken a position near the Volga River and set up camp before resuming their drive towards the city. In front of their position artillery pieces are in action bombarding enemy points along the east bank of the river. Note the 15cm heavy field howitzer is in its elevated position. These heavy field guns could hurl their destructive charge nearly 9 miles into the enemy lines.

(**Opposite, below**) On the outskirts of Stalingrad and these infantrymen pose for the camera, probably not aware of the terrible conflict that will soon ensue in and around the city.

(**Above**) In a captured Russian defensive position near the Volga and an MG34 machine gun can be seen mounted on an anti-aircraft tripod. Often when on a tripod the weapon would have an MG34 fifty-round basket drum magazine attached. Note the anti-aircraft ring sight which has also been fitted.

(**Opposite, above**) A mortar crew about to fire off a projectile from their 5cm leGrW 36 mortar. Although by 1942 this mortar was generally phased out, at Stalingrad it was still used widely by mortar crews and had already become a standard infantry weapon.

(**Opposite, below**) On the outskirts of Stalingrad and an infantryman keeps low in a field watching a burning Russian vehicle. He is armed with the Karbiner 98K rifle and wearing full battle kit. Note his *Zeltbahn* rolled up and attached to his 'Y' straps.

(**Above**) Infantry belonging to divisions of the 6th Army on the outskirts of Stalingrad in August 1942. It was the three infantry regiments which were the main fire and manoeuvre elements of a division. Their prime objectives were to take ground and hold positions. In Russia often two regiments would be deployed forward with one in reserve.

(**Above**) Two light MG34 gunners with their weapons on bipods overlooking Volga River.

(**Opposite, above**) An infantryman can be seen putting finishing touches to what probably is a captured Soviet shelter during operations along the Volga. The Germans built very similar shelters.

(**Opposite, below**) Romanian soldiers advancing along one of the many trenches around Stalingrad. There were two Romanian armies, the Third and Fourth, that were used to help protect the northern flank of the 6th Army as it battled its way through the city. However, poorly trained and lacking effective equipment the Romanians suffered massive losses, especially during the German relief operation codenamed Operation Uranus in November 1942.

(**Above**) Infantry taking cover behind a house in the outer suburbs of Stalingrad. They are all wearing, apart from one soldier, mosquito-proof head nets. Mosquitoes were a major problem for the soldiers in Russia, especially during the spring and summer periods.

(**Opposite, above**) Infantry in a dugout on the outskirts of Stalingrad. One of the soldiers appears to be poised to throw an Stg24 stick grenade, but probably this was staged for the photograph.

(**Opposite, below**) Outside Stalingrad and a rail hub has been destroyed by Soviet forces as they withdraw back across the River Volga. Locomotives and rolling stock that did not have time to be removed have also been destroyed.

(**Opposite, above**) An MG34 heavy machine gun crew during an enemy contact firing from a Lafette 34 tripod mount. Note the machine gunner using a long range optical site. His number two is feeding the ammunition belt through the weapon.

(**Opposite, below**) Along an anti-tank ditch and infantry await orders to begin their advance into the city. Initially, the attack into Stalingrad was expected to be a formality as it appeared the city was on the brink of collapse.

(**Above**) Two infantrymen pose at the entrance of their shelter. These bunkers were known by the troops as 'small houses'. They not only afforded protection against wind and rain, but were also very difficult to detect from the air. While they only gave minimal protection from bombardment they enabled troops to keep relatively warm at night.

(**Above**) The workhorse of the German artillery regiments was the 10.5cm l.FH18 seen here with camouflage applied to break up its distinctive shape from enemy surveillance. This weapon provided the division with an effective mobile base of fire. It was primarily the artillery regiments that were given the task of destroying enemy positions and fortified defences and conducting counter-battery fire before an armoured assault. These howitzers were used for initial assaults into the city.

(**Opposite, above**) A heavy MG gun troop with their 7.92cm MG34 advancing across some wasteland in the city.

(**Opposite, below**) Two members of a 7.92mm MG34 prepare to open fire on suspected enemy targets from inside a building. This light MG is being used from its bipod mount. With the bipod extended and the belt loaded, the machine gunner could quickly move the weapon from one position to another and put it into operation with deadly effect.

(**Above**) A rifleman can be seen drinking from his M31 canteen during a pause in the fighting. Note the soldier's steel helmet with a rubber ring strapped around it to insert camouflage. In this instance wheat has been used.

(**Opposite, above**) Infantry near a rail line at Gumrak just outside Stalingrad. The troops are in full battle kit and armed with the Karbiner 98k rifle. The rail lines into Stalingrad were vital to the survival of the 6th Army, as the bulk of their supplies and reinforcements were carried on them. As a result, hundreds of man-hours were spent by the German soldiers and pioneers building and repairing these vital lines.

(**Opposite, below**) A heavy MG34 Lafette machine gun position. These log shelters were typically built throughout the war by the German army to protect crews from enemy fire and the Russian weather. From these positions the machine gun troop were able to hold up entire enemy regiments with one single weapon.

Red Army soldiers have been captured between the Don and Volga River. Note the Russian 45mm anti-tank gun model 1937 nicknamed the Sorokapyatka abandoned at the side of the road.

Soldiers prepare to move a 7.5cm leIG.18 light infantry gun forward during fighting in the city. An infantry regiment's gun company normally comprised four 7.5cm and two 15cm infantry guns.

Two photographs showing a 5cm PaK 38 anti-tank gun concealed in an anti-tank gun nest, or Paknest during a pause in the fighting. An infantry regiment's anti-tank company normally had three platoons each with four PaKs.

A T-34 tank sits on its side after presumably falling off a walled ledge on the outskirts of Stalingrad. The T-34 was used extensively in the field resisting the German summer offensive in 1942. Later these tanks helped execute the double encirclement manoeuvre that cut off the German 6th Army at Stalingrad in December 1942.

(**Opposite, above**) Assault troops halt in a Stalingrad street. The soldiers are wearing a variety of kit. Note the light MG34 slung over the shoulder of one infantryman. Each attacking group always possessed an MG34 light machine gun, around which its base of fire was built.

(**Opposite, below**) A light MG machine gun troop in the bombed and blasted remains of Stalingrad pause before resuming their assault. The soldiers all wear a full kit, essential if they were to become isolated or cut off, which occurred often in the battle. Note that the MG34 has the 50-round basket drum magazine with a 250-round ammunition box nearby.

(**Above**) A forward observation post outside Stalingrad and these troops are surveying the battlefield from the edge of one of the many gullies in the fields around the city.

Inside a bomb crater and these two troop leaders are armed with the 9mm MP40 machine pistol. The troop leader carried the same basic equipment as a rifleman but had a pair of three-pocket machine pistol magazine pouches instead of the Karbiner 98K pouches.

A still from a propaganda film roll depicting Russian soldiers advancing through rubble defending and resisting as they go. Note that the assault soldier on the right is armed with a PPSh43 stock-extended sub-machine gun. These weapons were low-cost personal defence weapons mainly issued for reconnaissance units, vehicle crews and support personnel.

In the wasteland of Stalingrad and a knocked-out T-34 affords some protection to this 8cm sGrW 34 mortar crew. Two of the ammunition handlers or loaders can be seen holding the tripod to keep it steady and accurate when firing. This mortar earned a deadly reputation in line during the battle of Stalingrad and captured 34s were eagerly employed against the Germans.

A heavy MG34 Lafette machine gun troop on the advance through the rubble-strewn remains of Stalingrad. Each infantry battalion contained an MG company which fielded eight MG34 heavy machine guns on sustained fire-mounts.

A pair of exhausted soldiers pause in their march for a rest. One man is seen having a cigarette, while the other soldier seems to be trying to get some sleep while still sitting upright embracing his Karbiner 98k bolt-action rifle.

An NCO, more than likely a squad leader. He wears an M35 dispatch case on his right front and an MP40 magazine pouch on the left. The left pouch included a small pocket for a magazine-loading device. Note the rubber ring strap around his M35 steel helmet for inserting saplings for camouflage.

A soldier in a forward observation post using a pair of scissor binoculars to locate enemy positions.

In this photograph a German soldier moves through a captured trench and climbs over the dead Russian soldiers.

One of the many defensive positions built along the Don and Volga Rivers. Three soldiers can be seen smiling from the entrance of their shelter.

Three soldiers take cover near an entrance to a building during fighting in the city. The troop leader is armed with an MP40, while the other soldier is armed with a Karbiner 98k bolt action rifle complete with rifle grenade launcher, or *Schiessbecher* as it was commonly known, attached to the end of the weapon. *Schiessbecher* rifle grenade launchers were often used against infantry, fortifications and light armoured vehicles up to a range of 300 yards.

A soldier inside Stalingrad armed with an MP40. The gun was a very effective weapon and used extensively during the battle of Stalingrad. However, troops soon learned that it was prone to debris and brick dust, and the soldier often had to give the magazine a slap to restore operation.

A German squad leader armed with an MP40 escorts surrendered Russian soldiers out of a captured building. By the end of October Red Army positions had been pulverized into a few remaining pockets of resistance. Though General Paulus expressed confidence in winning the battle of Stalingrad, winter was fast approaching giving a new dimension to the conditions the soldiers would have to endure. German difficulties soon multiplied as news reached the 6th Army that large Russian formations were bearing down on Stalingrad.

Chapter III

Encircled

On the Don River the German XI Corps was given the task of supporting the left flank of the 6th Army. Here Russian forces of the 65th Army harassed the Germans and their allies. The Romanian 3rd Army, the Italian 8th Army and the Hungarian 2nd Amy were bearing the brunt. To support them the XLVII Panzer Corps, which included one German and one Romanian panzer division, was hurriedly dispatched. But many of the tanks had been lying for weeks camouflaged on the Don Front and mice had eaten into their electric wires. Only 39 out of the 104 panzers were able to move at first, and soon another 34 developed electrical problems and broke down, although a number were repaired and hastily sent to support the XI Corps. Moreover, many of the vehicles, especially in the Romanian 1st Panzer Division, were Czech Pz.Kpfw.35(t)s and 38(t)s, which were greatly inferior to the Russian tanks, and many were knocked out in their first contact.

The winter arrived suddenly in early November. On 2 November the Russians threw several new brigades across the Don at the Serafimovich bridgehead. Two days later the 6th Panzer Division and two infantry divisions were transferred from the English Channel coast to Army Group B, where they were to be employed as reserve forces behind the Italian 8th and Rumanian 3rd Armies.

Early on the morning of 19 November Russian forces began a large scale offensive around Stalingrad codenamed Operation Uranus. For miles, hundreds of tanks, artillery, and thousands of men burst onto the German line 100 miles north-west of Stalingrad, at the point where Rumanian troops made up most of the defensive formations. At the same time another thrust from the south was made to catch the German forces in a gigantic encirclement. The Rumanian soldiers were overwhelmed and Paulus could do nothing to help them. Instead he had to listen to reports of how Rumanian 4th Army defending the south of the city were being chased by Russian tanks and assaulted on the flanks by infantry and horse cavalry. Long range rocket and artillery barrages wore them down while they struggled through deep snow in arctic conditions. By 24 November, more than 30,000 Rumanian soldiers had capitulated.

Paulus's troops were now cut off and surrounded. Stalingrad now had a perimeter of 150 miles held grimly by nineteen German divisions, the Rumanian 20th and 1st Cavalry Divisions, and the Croatian 369th Regiment.

By 28 November the Russian encirclement of Stalingrad was completed. The Red Army had engineered a gigantic envelopment in the bend of the Don where more than 250,000 German and allied troops were marooned.

Inside the city, as a result of Operation Uranus, the 6th Army had also become trapped. Von Manstein assembled 6th, 17th and 23rd Panzer divisions, and the 16th Motorized Division, for a relief attempt on Stalingrad, while General Wolfram Freiherr von Richthofen's Luftflotte IV was given the responsibility for supplying the 6th Army by air-lift. The relief operation was named Winter Storm.

In the north, not far from the banks of the Volga, sat the 16th and 24th Panzer divisions. Fighting in the north-west were the 44th, 76th, and 384th divisions. In the west were remnants of the 376th Division, 3rd Motorized Division, 160th Motorized Division, and the 113th Infantry Division. In the south were 297th and 371st Infantry divisions and the 29th Motorized Division. In reserve, but trapped, were the 14th Panzer Division and the 9th Flak Division, two Rumanian divisions, and one regiment of Croatians. In the east, fighting inside the city itself, were the shattered and exhausted divisions of the 71st, 79th, 100th, 295th, 305th, and 389th. The men had come so close to winning the battle in October, but now, five weeks later, they were fighting for their lives and hoping Manstein would save them.

In early December Army Group Don began its preparations for putting together a task force to relieve the city. For the relief operation Manstein had managed to scrape together additional forces including the 11th and 6th Panzer divisions, the 62nd and 294th Infantry, a Luftwaffe division and a Gebirgsjäger division.

His relief attack began in earnest in the grey predawn light of 12 December, spearheaded by General Kirchner's LVII Panzer Corps, consisting of the 6th Panzer Division and the mauled 23rd Panzer Division supported by weak Rumanians forces. In the first few days the panzers steadily rolled forward, making good progress over the light snow. But despite a promising start, Manstein's forces were up against resilient opponents and his units were soon slowed down by strong Russian mechanized corps and tank brigades. By 21 December the 4th Panzer Army reported that it had advanced to within 30 miles of Stalingrad but that it could make no more progress against enemy resistance. Moreover, there was no more fuel for the vehicles.

On Christmas Eve, under incessant Russian attacks, the 4th Panzer Army was ordered to withdraw behind the Aksay River. As German units evacuated, Russian reinforcements poured across the Volga armed with fresh infantry and new tanks, and replaced the exhausted units holding the foothills on the western banks. From well-fortified positions the Russians continued to harass the trapped German soldiers.

As for Manstein's relief operation, it had ground to a halt in the snow.

A photograph of Field Marshal Erich von Manstein. Manstein was tasked to undertake the relief operation of Stalingrad, codenamed Winter Storm.

(**Opposite, above**) A Pz.Kpfw.III crosses a pontoon bridge during the Stalingrad relief effort. It was left to the 4th Panzer Army to wrench open a corridor to the German 6th Army. The German force was up against a number of strong Soviet armies that were tasked with the destruction of the encircled German forces and their offensive around the lower Chir River. Initially, German progress was good, but Soviet resistance soon slowed its advance down considerably.

(**Above**) During a pause in the fighting officers converse in a wooded area. In snow, soldiers found it necessary to apply white paint over their steel helmets. Initially, during the first winter of 1941, many troops did not attempt to apply their steel helmets with any type of white camouflage, leaving them field-grey. However, some did attempt to find a way to blend in with the local terrain. Chalk was useful and they applied this crudely over the entire helmet. But it was whitewash paint that became the most widely used form of winter camouflage.

(**Opposite, below**) An infantryman wearing a sheepskin coat standing next to some horses during Operation Winter Storm. The Stalingrad relief effort was spearheaded by General Kirchner's 57th Panzer-Corps, consisting of the 6th Panzer Division and the mauled 23rd Panzer Division.

(**Opposite, above**) A vehicle has become stuck in deep snow during the early stages of the Stalingrad relief operation. Other than tracked vehicles, wheeled forms of transportation were frequently immobilised due to the extreme weather conditions. This would hamper supplies to the front line and occasionally bring an advance to a stall.

(**Above**) An interesting photograph showing two Luftwaffe FlaK crew wearing animal-skin greatcoats standing beside their emplaced 2cm FlaK30. This FlaK gun weighed some 770kg and had an effective ceiling range of 2,200 metres against aerial targets.

(**Opposite, below**) Russian soldiers are captured hiding under a railway bridge during the relief operation. Initially the German drive towards Stalingrad went well with a number of Red Army units being surrounded, captured or destroyed.

(**Above**) Infantrymen of the Army Group Don relief effort trudge through snow during operations against Soviet forces. On their backs they show the infantryman's combat equipment, which generally consisted of shelter quarter, canteen, bread bag, gas mask canister and entrenching tool. Slung over their shoulder is the Kar98 bolt-action rifle.

(**Opposite, above**) Out in the field is a six-barrelled Nebelwerfer 41 multiple rocket launcher. To conceal the weapon the crew have applied foliage over the rocket tubes and ammunition cases, which can be seen dangerously placed beneath the launcher. After the crew had loaded and aimed the launcher, they would take cover a few metres away and fire the Nebelwerfer by an electric wire.

(**Opposite, below**) Two troops pulling a sled, probably containing ammunition. Both the soldiers are wearing the shapeless two-piece snowsuit comprising a snow jacket and matching trousers. The jacket was buttoned all the way down the front with white painted buttons. It had a large white hood, which could easily be pulled over the steel helmet. The hood not only helped conceal the headgear if it had not already received any type of winter covering, but also afforded protection to the back of the wearer's neck and to the ears. The trousers were also shapeless and were tucked into the boots.

Two photographs showing a gun crew wearing the two-piece snow suit preparing their whitewashed 7.5cm Geb36 for action during winter operations in January 1943. With the relief effort for Stalingrad in tatters Manstein had no choice but to retreat to Kotelnikovo on 29 December, leaving more than 300,000 soldiers encircled in and around Stalingrad to their fate. During Manstein's retreat artillery crews attempted to slow the enemy's advance, to prepare better defensive positions and avoid being outflanked and encircled.

A soldier is donning his winter whites before resuming his daily duties on the battlefield. Note how dirty his trousers have become.

(**Opposite, above**) Troops prepare to move out of a village as the 1st Panzer Army is evacuated through Rostov in January 1943.

(**Above**) Dressed in their familiar winter smocks, German troops are photographed in a slit trench in the snow. Shelter for the soldiers was often at a premium, especially when evacuating a position. Out in the snow, soldiers were compelled not only to build various forms of shelter to combat the arctic temperatures, but to protect themselves against enemy fire.

(**Opposite, below**) Infantry on the march during the 'Winter Storm' relief operation in December 1942. The soldiers pass a destroyed Russian vehicle which is still on fire.

(**Opposite, above**) A variety of vehicles including a sidecar combination and a lorry towing a whitewashed 7.5cm PaK 40 during the relief operation. Preparing artillery, FlaK and PaK guns for action on the battlefield relied heavily on various light and heavy vehicles for transportation. Maintaining the momentum of an advance was vital to success and without transport the whole advance would stall.

(**Opposite, below**) Out in the snow a heavy MG34 troop can be seen during an enemy action in January 1943. A well-positioned MG34 machine gunner was quite capable of holding up attacking infantry many times their number. In fact, just a couple of well-sighted adequately-supplied machine guns could hold up an entire attacking unit on a frontage of 5 miles or more.

(**Above**) The first of two photographs showing a PaK 40 out in the snow being prepared for action. The effectiveness of the PaK 40 in Russia made the gun very popular, but there were never enough to meet the ever-increasing demand in the east.

(**Opposite, above**) Throughout its life on the battlefield the PaK 40 was a powerful and deadly weapon, especially in the hands of well-trained anti-tank gunners. However, because of the weight of the weapon it led to instances where gun crews reluctantly abandoned their precious PaK 40 because they could not manhandle them in bad ground conditions caused by the winter snow or spring thaw.

(**Above**) Dressed in winter smock a German soldier is photographed next to his shelter in the snow. Shelter for the soldiers was often at a premium, especially when evacuating a position.

(**Opposite, below**) Here the crew of a whitewashed 21cm Mrs18 can be seen during a lull in the fighting. Note the wheels of the gun are slightly raised. This was done to allow the gun full 360-degree traverse of fire. Pieces of timber are scattered beside the gun, used by the crew to prevent it sinking in the soft ground.

(**Opposite, above**) During 'Winter Storm' and a whitewashed Pz.Kpfw.III supports infantry on the march across a snowy field in December 1942. It was Hoth's Fourth Panzer Army's LVII Panzer Corps that began its north-eastward drive toward the Stalingrad pocket. The 6th and 23rd Panzer Divisions made good progress, surprising the Red Army and threatening the rear of Soviet 51st Army. What followed was a rapid drive by the Germans, with some units reporting they had covered 30 miles in a single day. But it did not take long until the Russians began stiffening resistance and blocking Manstein's spearheads.

(**Opposite, below**) Three soldiers inside a trench. They all wear the early snow suit. Front-line German troops were normally issued with colour armbands, as seen here, enabling them to distinguish between friend and foe.

(**Above**) Two soldiers clad in two-piece snow camouflage suits are seen here on patrol. The white camouflage smocks were a popular item of clothing, and soldiers tended to wear them night and day for weeks on end. Soon they became filthy, thus defeating the objective of the white camouflage.

A commanding officer can be seen with his troops. The soldiers are all wearing their 'winter whites' and a number of them can be seen with whitewashed M35 steel helmets. Within two weeks of the relief effort, Russian forces were pushing back Manstein's forces, with infantry and armoured units struggling to maintain cohesion against overwhelming enemy forces.

Infantry converse next to a support truck. Even at this period of the war some vehicles still lacked white camouflage paint. Short supplies in some sectors of the front meant that crews often had to travel great distances in the snow and risk enemy attack. Note that only one soldier is wearing the whitewashed winter outfit, the others wearing the standard *Landser* greatcoat.

A whitewashed Tiger tank can be seen halted in the snow with two support vehicles and troops halted next to it. By Christmas Eve it had been reported that the 4th Panzer Army was in full retreat and unable to break through to the 6th Army. This caused the whole of the 'Winter Storm' relief operation to collapse and Army Group Don to go back on the defensive.

Infantry from Manstein's relief operation are now in full retreat following the collapse of the operation. In this photograph the men have congregated together to prepare to move out. By the end of 1942, the distance between the German 6th Army entombed in Stalingrad and the German formations outside the city was around 40 miles. By this period units in the area had been severely weakened, and this allowed Soviet forces to continue efforts to cut off German forces in the Caucasus.

A photograph showing supplies for Stalingrad by Junker 52 transport plane. It was Richthofen's Luftflotte 4 that was tasked to supply Stalingrad by air and to carry out air supply missions in support of the 6th Army and other depleted forces around the city. Richthofen's transport fleet comprised the 1st (staff), 50th, 102nd, 172nd, and 900th Special Purposes Bomber Wings, equipped with Ju 52s, and the Fifth Special Purpose Bomber Wing, equipped with He-111s.

Chapter IV

Destruction of the 6th Army

In the pocket and inside Stalingrad itself the Russians waged a relentless battle of attrition. Paulus pleaded to Manstein that his army was 'on the brink of extinction'. Stalingrad, he said had become a graveyard. Hitler was warned about the dire situation, but the Führer believed the 6th Army was safe inside its 'fortress' and could hold out until the spring. He had ordered Göring to increase the air supply to 300 tons a day and thought that this would be enough, but the situation was far worse than Hitler realised. The 6th Army was starving to death. On 26 December the daily bread ration was reduced to 120 grams, and then halved. There were stories of soldiers seen picking the oats out of their excrement, and eating the flesh from the bodies of their dead comrades before they froze. Many were now too weak to dig in. They would simply huddle behind heaped snow, numb with cold, and wait for the inevitability of either freezing to death or being killed by a sniper.

The Red Army now prepared to wipe out the Germans in Stalingrad. General Hoth's 4th Panzer Army did what it could to help by fighting some desperate battles against superior Russian forces to try to keep open a corridor through to the city. At its nearest point leading units were still only 20 miles from the 6th Army perimeter, but the Red Army had by now driven the main force back some 60 miles to Kotelnikovo.

The Russians were fully aware that the Germans were still powerful within the pocket, in spite of their weakened condition, and the battles had been equally costly for the Russians. General Rokossovsky, commander of the Don Front, called upon the Germans to surrender. On the morning of 8 January 1943, three Russian representatives carrying a white flag walked through the German lines and delivered the ultimatum to Paulus. It stated that unless the Germans ceased hostilities and surrendered by ten o'clock the next morning, 'the Red Army and Air Force will be compelled to wipe out the surrounded German troops.' Paulus submitted the Russian ultimatum to Hitler and pleaded for freedom of action. The Führer refused and told Paulus it was imperative that his army held out for as long as possible, as it was helping the entire front. Plans were being drawn up for a new relief expedition and three new panzer divisions were being moved from France, but they would not arrive until February. Paulus now knew that it would take a miracle to save the 6th Army.

On 10 January the Russians began a massive attack to wipe out the Germans and their allies in the pocket. The German 376th and 384th divisions were engulfed by the Red Army and totally annihilated. In the south-west the German 29th Motorized and 3rd Motorized division tried to hold but were mercilessly battered by Russian infantry supported by armour. The 3rd Motorized Division was forced to withdraw across the Rossoshka River with serious losses. The 29th Motorized Division, after fighting off heavy attacks, retreated, leaving the steppe littered with burning vehicles and corpses. The Hungarian 7th Division endured a hideous battle which resulted in their total destruction. The confusion was such that men often ran the wrong way, straight into the enemy, only to be mown down or captured and killed. Within a week, the Hungarians had lost 96,000 killed, wounded or missing. The German 76th Division had now been reduced from 10,000 men to only 600. The Red Army had reduced the western side of the pocket to approximately 250 square miles, and was within 5 miles of Paulus's headquarters. Gumrak airfield and Stalingrad were no more than 10 miles away.

To defend these western approaches and form a defensive line north to south in front of Stalingrad, the 113th and 297th divisions, 14th Panzer and 9th Flak divisions, along with exhausted remnants of six other divisions were sent into the 20-mile defence line. For five long days the troops shivered and died of exposure on the steppe, too weak to dig a fox-hole. Most just sat around, huddling together for warmth, waiting for the next artillery bombardment.

As the pocket shrunk the Red Army edged ever closer to Stalingrad from the west. Paulus and his staff evacuated their headquarters and retreated within Stalingrad to set up a new command. By 17 January the Russians reported that they had destroyed some 1,260 pillboxes and fortified dugouts, including 75 heavily defended observation posts and 317 gun emplacements. They had also captured or destroyed 400 aircraft, 6,600 tanks, and around 16,000 trucks. Some 25,000 Germans had been killed and several thousand prisoners taken, many of whom were Rumanians.

On 22 January Gumrak, the last airfield, fell as the Russians tore a 3-mile gap in the south-western sector. With no fuel and a lack of guns and ammunition, the 6th Army was unable to close the gap. The following day the Red Army broke through the western perimeter and leading units penetrated German positions all the way to the tractor works. The Russian drive into Stalingrad cut the pocket in two and isolated the XI Corps to the north. A weary and exhausted Paulus reported that there were more than 12,000 unattended wounded lying in the streets or inside ruined buildings. Hitler ordered Paulus not to surrender under any circumstances and instructed him to give food only to those capable of fighting.

Despair and dread gripped the German soldiers inside Stalingrad. Paulus's army was now broken into two pockets and conditions were appalling. The general himself was now suffering from dysentery and close to nervous breakdown. His headquarters was now situated in the ruins of a large department store in Red Square, defended by what was left of General Hartmann's 71st Infantry Division.

While the remains of 6th Army was being blown to pieces, Hitler showered promotions on its senior officers. He promoted Paulus to field marshal, knowing that no German of that rank had ever surrendered. Perhaps unaware of his Führer's ulterior motive, the newly decorated field marshal sent a dignified response of his allegiance to Hitler: 'On the anniversary of your accession to power, the 6th Army sends greetings to its Führer. The swastika flag still flutters over Stalingrad. Should our struggle be an example to present and future generations never to surrender, even when all hope is gone, then Germany will be victorious. Heil, Mein Führer!'

During that day fighting intensified as Red Army forces began overwhelming the last German defensive positions. The 76th Infantry Division was surrounded and forced to surrender. Near railway station No. 1, the headquarters of the XIV Panzer Corps was also compelled to capitulate. In the northern pocket, Russian T-34s had smashed their way through hundreds of German troops. Within a matter of hours the command bunkers of the VIII and LI corps were captured. Generals Seydlitz-Kurzbach, Heitz, and five other generals reluctantly surrendered. The Russians then attacked the 71st Infantry and during the street fighting General Hartmann was killed. Soviet troops were also closing in on Paulus's command post.

On the morning of 31 January at 6.15, the radio operator in Paulus's headquarters sent a message: 'The Russians are at the door. We are preparing to destroy the radio equipment.' The radio then went dead. Minutes later a German officer climbed out of the command post and waved a white flag to approaching Russian soldiers. Paulus had surrendered.

Two days later, at 8.40 in the morning of 2 February, the last German pocket in Stalingrad surrendered. General Strecker's XI Corps had fought courageously for days. As Strecker's exhausted and starved men shuffled pitifully through the snow into captivity, the Russians rejoiced. The battle of Stalingrad, the longest and bloodiest battle of the war, had finally ended.

Aftermath

The losses sustained at Stalingrad were immense on both sides. Germany's allies had lost more troops than the Germans themselves. The Rumanians had lost 173,000 killed, wounded, and missing, of which a quarter had perished through malnutrition and the cold. The Croatian expeditionary force had been totally destroyed, including the 369th Regiment. The Italians had lost 115,000 dead and wounded, with 66,000 missing, of which many drowned in the semi-frozen rivers that had cracked open under the weight of retreating soldiers. As for the Germans, some 150,000 were killed, with 91,000 being taken into captivity, many of whom were never to see their homeland again. During the fighting some 30,000 wounded were flown out of the ravaged city.

Russian losses were much higher. Although figures vary, at least 750,000 Red Army troops were killed or wounded. Of the buildings of Stalingrad, 99 per cent were destroyed, and of the 500,000 inhabitants of the city, only 1,500 remained to endure the horror, with many being caught-up and killed in the battle.

Although the Russians paid a high price, victory was theirs. The banks of the Don and the Volga were now littered with the dead, and the ambitions of the once vaunted 6th Army had been destroyed. Although Hitler said that the 6th Army had provided a valuable service by tying down 750,000 enemy troops, the loss of the campaign marked the turning point of the war. Never again was Hitler to launch a major offensive in Russia. He was now faced with a relentlessly growing and improving Red Army.

Two MG42 machine gunners can be seen vacating their shelter in early January 1943 during the last weeks of the battle of Stalingrad.

While 6th Army continued resisting inside the besieged city, outside Stalingrad units carried on fighting trying to help relieve the pressure on the soldiers trapped inside. Here three soldiers clad in their winter whites can be seen in a slit trench directing their weapons at a disabled Russian tank.

A photograph has captured the moment a sIG.33 artillery gun is fired during operations outside Stalingrad. The soldiers are wearing the snow overall. This white garment was an early piece of snow clothing which covered the entire service uniform. It was shapeless, had buttons right down the front, a deep collar, an attached hood and long sleeves. The infantryman's leather belt and personal equipment was worn attached around the outside.

A light MG34 machine gunner positioned in the snow during the last weeks of the battle of Stalingrad in January 1943.

Soldiers are using spades in the snow to clear a path for traffic to drive through. The soldiers are being helped by a woman. During the war the Wehrmacht made substantial use of personnel from the Soviet Union. They often ran errands, brought food and dug anti-tank ditches. Despite the 6th Army beinging trapped inside Stalingrad, German troops and their Allies continued fighting outside the city tying down a significant number of Soviet forces.

A Russian T-34 sits abandoned in the snow outside Stalingrad. In early January 1943 a huge Russian offensive was unleashed squeezing the pocket at Stalingrad from west to east. The Soviets were met by determined German resistance and counter-attacks.

Sited outside near the Volga is a whitewashed 8.8cm flak gun position. The 8.8cm FlaK was often difficult to make out at long distances, especially when whitewashed.

A Russian ZiS-2 57-mm anti-tank gun has been positioned in one of the factory buildings for a fire mission.

Taken from a film still, a German soldier raises a white flag of surrender to Soviet troops. By the end of January 1943 the southern pocket in Stalingrad collapsed and there were wholesale surrenders by units that had either run out of ammunition or were starving to death.

On 31 January 1943 Field Marshal von Paulus finally surrendered the remains of 6th Army that were still holding on inside Stalingrad. Here an exhausted and pale von Paulus and two members of his staff are being led from the Univermag Department Store, his headquarters, to be taken to 64th Army Headquarters in Beketovka south of Stalingrad for interrogation.

General Elder von Daniels of the 6th Army being escorted away for questioning. General von Daniels was commander of the 376th Infantry Division. The division incurred horrendous casualties and by the end of the battle was virtually destroyed. Note they pass a dead German soldier. In the last weeks of the battle the dead were left frozen where they lay.

A column of prisoners from the 6th Army shuffle along a snowy road following their surrender. These men were totally demoralised after 199 days of brutal combat. Virtually all were marched off to prison camps either suffering from exhaustion or frostbite; many collapsed and died on the way.

Fatigued German prisoners are given a light for their cigarettes by a Russian soldier. As a rule, in the first weeks of their captivity the Germans were treated without sympathy and thousands perished.

More prisoners from the 6th Army. One soldier can be seen cutting into some bread, a rare find in the last days of the battle. This photograph appears to have been taken somewhere on the frozen banks of the Volga. Behind the men are dugouts in the bluff's side. For weeks the exhausted remnants of six divisions manned a 20-mile defence line along the Volga to prevent Soviet crossings.

A Russian unit cross no man's land inside the destroyed city following the 6th Army's surrender.

The defeated made ready their captivity by wrapping themselves with rags and other items of uniform clothing. The Russian's took many photographs of the demoralised prisoners which were widely published in Soviet newspapers to demonstrate that the Germans were not invincible.

Appendix

Order of Battle

6th Army – 8 June 1942

XVII
294 Infantry Division

XXIX
75 Infantry Division   57 Infantry Division
168 Infantry Division

LI
44 Infantry Division   71 Infantry Division
297 Infantry Division   62 Infantry Division

VIII
336 Infantry Division   305 Infantry Division
113 Infantry Division   79 Infantry Division

XXXX (mot.)
23 Panzer Division   3 Panzer Division

III (mot.)
60 Infantry Division (mot.)   376 Infantry Division
22 Panzer Division   108 Infantry Division
16 Panzer Division   389 Infantry Division
14 Panzer Division

6th Army – 24 June 1942

XVII
294 Infantry Division   113 Infantry Division
79 Infantry Division

XXIX
75 Infantry Division   57 Infantry Division
168 Infantry Division

VIII
376 Infantry Division   305 Infantry Division
389 Infantry Division

XXXX (mot.)
23 Panzer Division   336 Infantry Division
3 Panzer Division   100 (leichte) Infantry Division
29 Infantry Division (mot.)   Infantry Regiment 369 (Kroat.)

6th Army – 4 July 1942

XVII
294 Infantry Division   113 Infantry Division
79 Infantry Division

XXIX
75 Infantry Division   57 Infantry Division
168 Infantry Division

LI
44 Infantry Division   71 Infantry Division
297 Infantry Division   62 Infantry Division

VIII
389 Infantry Division   305 Infantry Division
376 Infantry Division

XXXX AK (mot.)
23 Panzer Division   29 Infantry Division (mot.)
3 Panzer Division   376 Infantry Division
100 (leichte) Infantry Division   108 Infantry Division
336 Infantry Division   389 Infantry Division

6th Army – 5 August 1942

XVII
79 Infantry Division   3 Infantry Division 'Celere'

XIV (mot.)
60 Infantry Division (mot.)   3 Infantry Division (mot.)
16 Panzer Division

LI
44 Infantry Division   295 Infantry Division

VIII
384 Infantry Division   305 Infantry Division
376 Infantry Division   113 Infantry Division

XXIV
24 Panzer Division   71 Infantry Division
297 Infantry Division   76 Infantry Division

6th Army – 12 August 1942

XVII
79 Infantry Division   113 Infantry Division
3 Infantry Division 'Celere'   Bers. Reg. 6
22 Panzer Division

XIV Panzer Korps
60 Infantry Division (mot.)   3 Infantry Division (mot.)
16 Panzer Division

LI
    44 Infantry Division   71 Infantry Division
XI
    100 Jäger Division   Infantry Regiment 369 (Kroat.)
VIII
    384 Infantry Division   305 Infantry Division
    376 Infantry Division   389 Infantry Division
XXIV Panzer Korps
    16 Infantry Division (mot.)   295 Infantry Division

6th Army – 2 September 1942

XVII
    79 Infantry Division   22 Panzer Division
    113 Infantry Division
XIV Panzer Korps
    60 Infantry Division (mot.)   3 Infantry Division (mot.)
    16 Panzer Division   295 Infantry Division
LI
    71 Infantry Division   76 Infantry Division
VIII
    384 Infantry Division   305 Infantry Division
    389 Infantry Division
XI
    44 Infantry Division   376 Infantry Division
    100 Jäger Division

6th Army – 8 October 1942

VIII rum. [Rumania]
    14 Infantry Division (rum.)   6 Infantry Division (rum.)
    5 Infantry Division (rum.)   13 Infantry Division (rum.)
    1 Panzer Division (rum.)   1 Cavalry Division (rum.)
XIV Panzer Korps
    60 Infantry Division (mot.)   3 Infantry Division (mot.)
    16 Panzer Division   94 Infantry Division
LI
    389 Infantry Division   24 Panzer Division
    100 Jäger Division   295 Infantry Division
VIII
    113 Infantry Division   305 Infantry Division

XI

44 Infantry Division
384 Infantry Division
376 Infantry Division

71 Infantry Division
76 Infantry Division

6th Army – 19 November 1942

IV Corps

29 (Mot.) Infantry Division
297 Infantry Division

371 Infantry Division

VII Corps

76 Infantry Division

113 Infantry Division

XI Corps

44 Infantry Division
376 Infantry Division

384 Infantry Division

XIV Panzer Corps

3 (Mot.) Infantry Division
60 (Mot.) Infantry Division

16 Panzer-Division

LI Corps

71 Infantry Division
79 Infantry Division
94 Infantry Division
100 Jäger-Division
295 Infantry Division
305 Infantry Division
389 Infantry Division
14 Panzer Division
24 Panzer Division
9 Flak Division
51 Mortar Regiment
53 Mortar Regiment
2 Nebelwerfer Regiment
30 Nebelwerfer Regiment

4 Artillery Regiment
46 Artillery Regiment
64 Artillery Regiment
70 Artillery Regiment
54 Artillery Battalion
616 Artillery Battalion
627 Artillery Battalion
849 Artillery Battalion
49 Heavy Artillery Battalion
101 Heavy Artillery Battalion
733 Heavy Artillery Battalion
6 Pioneer Battalion
41 Pioneer Battalion

Soviet Order of Battle – 17 July 1942

64th Army
29th Infantry Division
112th Infantry Division
214th Infantry Division
229th Infantry Division
783rd Infantry Regiment

804th Infantry Regiment
66th (Motorised) Naval Infantry Brigade
154th (Motorised) Naval Infantry Brigade
40th Armoured Brigade
137th Armoured Brigade
5 Heavy Tanks

Soviet Order of Battle – October 1942

62nd Army
10th NKVD Rifle Division
2 × infantry brigades
13th Guards Rifle Division
34th Guards Regiment
39th Guards Regiment
42nd Guards Regiment
35th Guards Rifle Division
37th Guards Rifle Division
1st Guards Rifle Regiment
114th Guards Rifle Regiment
117th Guards Rifle Regiment
39th Guards Rifle Division
117th Guards Rifle Regiment
118th Guards Rifle Regiment
45th Rifle Division
95th Rifle Division
161st Rifle Regiment
241st Rifle Regiment
112th Rifle Division
416th Rifle Regiment

524th Rifle Regiment
138th Rifle Division
650th Rifle Regiment
193rd Rifle Division
685th Rifle Regiment
196th Rifle Division
244th Rifle Division
284th (Siberian) Rifle Division
308th (Siberian) Rifle Division
117th Rifle Regiment
84th Tank Brigade
137th Tank Brigade
189th Tank Brigade
92nd Naval Infantry Brigade
42nd Special Brigade
115th Special Brigade
124th Special Brigade
140th Special Brigade
160th Special Brigade
8th Air Army

Notes

Notes

Notes

Notes

Notes